S0-CAZ-645

If something goes wrong,
if a butterfly attacks you
and spoils your swing...

remember... tennis
is a challenging sport.

The Second Serve

*Or the Best Seat in the House

This is a good serve; it isn't what you paid to learn, but it goes in better than the one you just tried. First concentrate on the possibility of your opponent going blind. If that doesn't work, remember that this serve is more effective if used as a first serve against advanced players because (1) they will not believe it, (2) they really don't know how to hit it, and (3) it's been years since they have seen anything like it. However, after you win a few points with this serve, you will notice that your opponent will remember he promised to play someone else that day.

The second serve is also called the Best Seat in the House. You spend so much time loving what you've done, you don't have time to play too. Instead of hitting the ball and moving to a position in the center of the court or at base line, you stand around and watch your shot. Instead of following your serve in, you stop after you hit the ball, look up stretching to see where the ball is landing. The ball is good! Your opponent returns it, and you, in the best seat in the house, watch it admiringly.

Got to get it in.

Ready.

Toss.

See the ball?

Hit it.

Follow through.

Watch your opponent smile.   Here it comes.

There it goes.

I paid $125 for this racket. and I have a closet full of tennis shirts and drawers and drawers packed with tennis shorts, socks, jocks.

I once played an amazing singles match with Bobby Riggs. Being a celebrity, he gave me a good handicap. He put on a Fat Albert suit that made him weigh about four hundred pounds. I figured that was a good handicap—one that would throw off his serve anyway, if not his backhand.

He served and won the first game.

I served and lost my serve. Bobby was ahead 2–love.

Then, to be fair, he increased his handicap by having food placed all over the court (Fat Albert eats a lot). He had to leap over six turkeys, eight roast beefs, five hams, and twenty cream pies scattered on his side of the court. I gained a few points when my shots hit the cream pies. The ball didn't bounce, so Bobby couldn't return it. But he won the set anyway.

I served again, but not before I added a bowl of All Bran to the court. I missed. Bobby was winning 4–love.

I then insisted that a female come on the court, that Bobby hold her hand, toss the ball with his racket hand and, after the serve, kiss her. I also demanded that when I served, he return with his left hand, kiss the girl, and switch the racket to his right hand.

I lost the serve and the set 6–love.

I think my mistake was putting the girl out there. At his age, her presence did not break his concentration.

The Forehand

*Or Do I Have to Do two in a Row?

I'll get to the forehand right away and skip the ready position because, even though you are **not** ready, you know how to **look** ready, which is probably your best stroke.

When you see the ball coming, don't pull your racket back right away (even though you paid eight to twenty dollars a half-hour to have someone yell this at you). Have a little conversation with yourself: "Gee, he hit it! It's coming at me! Oh God."

By the time you are finished chatting with yourself, the ball is coming over the net. Pull the racket back just as the ball is almost upon you. As the racket goes back, the ball (which won't wait) follows it. To compensate for any lateness, quickly bend your wrist, look back, lean back, and hit forward. You may mis-hit but don't throw your racket into the nearest litter barrel. Throw yourself in.

Ready.

How'd he do that?

Step forward,
arch the body back and
give myself more time.

Hah!

The Open Body Forehand

This is a wonderful shot and one you can be proud of. On this one, you don't turn your body at all. Just pull the racket back, keeping an eye on where you are going to hit it. Your follow-through is looking under your arm as the ball laughs itself into the fence behind you.

Step forward.   Hold the racket back.

Bend the knees.
Keep wrist straight.

Where is the ball going?
Wait! Come back, come back...

The Stiff Leg Forehand

Never bend your legs during this shot—only after you've blown it.

You see the ball coming. It's coming fast and you wonder how he got it so low, and so fast, and you have started to swing and mentally you know it won't go over the net.

It's low and you keep
your eye on it, beginning
your "top spin" stroke.

That's it!! Turn the wrist without any arm motion. An open mouth may help get it back over.

Your knees are bent only because you are frozen
by the speed of the ball. But you don't even turn sideways
because you think you don't have time.

Rise on the toes to help get the ball higher.
Add body twisting to the wrist twisting.

If the ball is heading toward the net—
help it over by raising the racket, twisting the body
some more, and keeping the mouth open.

I've lost in doubles to some of the greatest players in the world. Alan King and I played Pancho Gonzalez and Pancho Segura. It gives me a great deal of pain to tell you this, but the only way that we would play them (and it was Alan's suggestion, not mine), was if they tied their shoes together. That way, we thought, we could minimize the impact of their forehand. Pancho Gonzalez tied the laces of his left shoe to Pancho Segura's right shoe. Segura used his left hand and Gonzalez used his right, so they looked like Siamese twins.

Alan and I lost 6–1. We took the one game by calling a foot fault on Gonzalez because Segura's foot was in on the court. Not only did they whip us but they looked funny doing it.

The Backhand

*Or Entertaining Your Pro During a Lesson

When you're stuck with a tennis complex, take a look at some of the thousands of backhands. Thousands of them, I tell you. Every pro will say, knowing he is telling one of the biggest lies ever told, "The backhand is a natural stroke." You never had this much trouble learning how to eat or blink your eyes, and you never shuddered in fear when turning over in bed. So don't believe that natural-stroke stuff. The backhand is like a bad date—you don't want to go through with it, but since you have to, the sooner it's over, the better.

Now you never hit it in front, never. Never when it's away from you, and you seldom turn the body. Wait until the ball is crawling up on you, attacking you, trying to bite you, trying to eat you. Yes, it's going to hurt you. **Then** swing at it to get it away from you.

The body leans backward, supported by a straight back leg; the other leg is up off the ground. The neck is also stretching back to get away from the thing. The arms are raised, elbows bent close to the body, and the racket arm straightened out to hit it away.

This stroke, after the ball goes anywhere but in, is usually followed by some primitive vocal sounds. At which point you can give a demonstration of a perfect backhand hitting an imaginary ball. Like the prizefighter, after being knocked out, who goes back to his dressing room and practices ducking.

I'm ready
—alert
but calm.

Shrewdly I notice
that it's a backhand.

I don't want a backhand,
but I keep my face
a cool mask.

It's bouncing high
and coming up at me.

But I lean back
so I can have more time.

The net
decides to play.

After missing,
I show opponent how to do it.

The Topspin Backhand

Racket back.
Step Forward.

Hi. I missed
the whole ball.

The Late Backhand

The ball tries to get past me.

I change my mind and "cool it" off the court.

The Flick Backhand

Racket is back.

The ball is in sight.   Flick.

I was scheduled to play Don Budge and Ross Martin in the Pro Celebrity Tournament. I was already warming up with my pro partner, Fred Stolle, when Budge walked by. He stopped at the edge of the court and watched while I hit a backhand with what I believed to be my finest form. He looked at me very carefully and said, "Do you prefer that to a backhand?"

Well, needless to say, my insecurity got the best of me and I asked him what I was doing wrong. Said Budge, "You're on the court."

"Well," I said, "How far off should I get?"

"Have you ever tried fishing?" he asked.

The Lob

*How to Play Baseball on the Tennis Court

The lob is a fascinating shot when it is coming toward you. It is so pretty, you will want to stare at it to see how high it will go. By the time you find out, it has turned into a bullet.

The tendency, when you see the lob flying, is to reach up and catch it with a mitt. Resist the urge, unless a scout for the Yankees is in the stands, in which case, go ahead and catch it and throw it fast to home plate.

This looks like a lob.   **It is a lob.**

Oh God. It's so high and it's going to bounce in.

It's coming down.

Elegantly, I make it.

Now I hit down.

[EXPLETIVE DELETED]

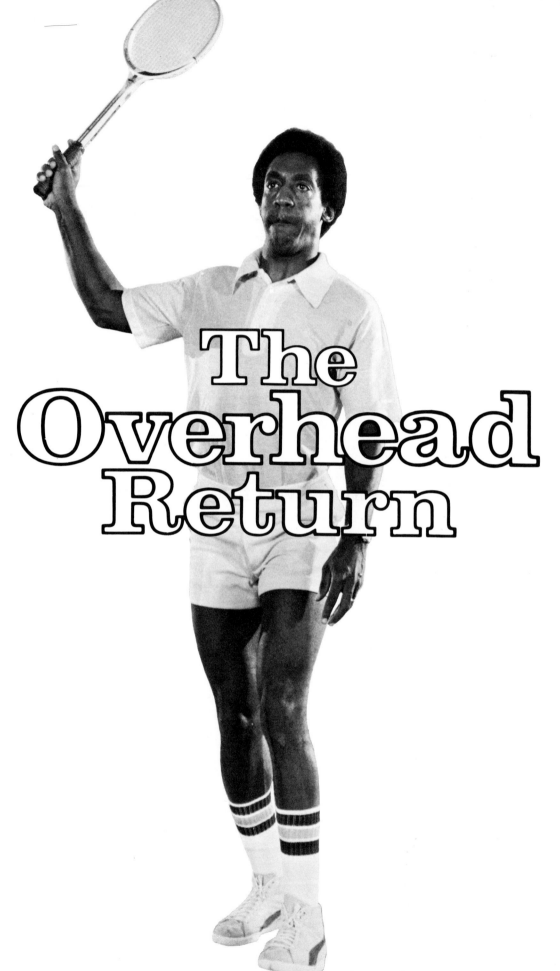

The Overhead Return

*Or Ending the Game Early

This is also a difficult shot to execute. If you want to look good returning it, invent your own stroke: make something up, use your imagination. Constant application of brand-new strokes will free the court for the next couple.

Ah, yes.
It's a high shot.
Not much of a problem.

But it's so high I don't
want to knock it out
by hitting it flat.

So I put a little homemade twist of the wrist on it.

And send it...

...into the net and stab myself with my follow-through.

One of the most embarrassing moments I've ever had happened during my second year of tennis playing. A gentleman on the elevator of the Las Vegas Hilton Hotel said hello to me. I had my tennis clothes on; I was going down to the court. He told me his name, which I forgot immediately because I thought he was just some guy on the elevator. He asked me how the courts were and I said the courts were fine, and he asked me if I was going down to play and I said yes. He said, "I'd like to come down and play with you." And I said, "Fine, come down." (I play with anybody because—well—I just love to play).

The man looked to be fifty years old. Nice-looking, kinda thin. I went down, talked with the pro, told him I had a game and booked the court. All I can remember from the set we played was that this man returned everything I hit. I realized that he could hit after I warmed up with him, but I figured there must be some things that he couldn't hit. But the man was always there, even on my little dink shots that dropped over the net. He had a wonderful way of surprising me with a lob. It seemed that no matter where I went, a lob was going over my head. Now at this particular time, I had not learned an important thing about the lob. You see, you can better your chances of getting a ball that's been lobbed over your head if you (1) realize that it is a lob, (2) do not stand there and watch it. I was just amazed at the lob and just wanted to stand there to see how high it would go. And then, as it reached its peak, I would turn around and run after it, which, of course, worked to my disadvantage. Well, needless to say, the man won the set, 6–love. I was so tired chasing all those lobs I was glad it was over. He must have lobbed about seven hundred times; each time I would chase it down and do some ridiculous thing like running with my back turned to him, catching the ball as it bounced away from me, hitting it back over my shoulder with the racket following through, hitting myself in the face. The ball would go back on his court. He would then hit something soft to me (nothing he hit was hard). I would hit back some dink way much like a ping-pong player. I would then rush to the net because volleying was my strongest point—so I thought. And then, this lob would show up again and there I was running back again, watching the ball go up in the air and saying to myself things like "That's a lob."

So when I finished this 6–love set, it was three o'clock in the afternoon. People had gathered around and I thought it was their interest in Bill Cosby. Later I learned that I had been making a fool of myself with Frank Parker, who for many years ranked in the top ten of the U.S. Lawn Association and won Forest Hills in 1944. I'm happy to say that Frank Parker and I teamed up in July 1974 and won the Pro Celebrity Tennis Match in Chicago. We beat Tony Trabert and Charlton Heston, but I can never forget the day Frank beat me, 6–love.

My
Favorite
Shots

Bending the knees.

Body turned sideways,
looking over shoulder.

Returning a shot
without moving the feet.

Saving energy.

Making up
my own strokes.

Following through
on the front leg
—racket extended.

Looking brilliant
after blowing each point.

Well, that's it. I hope all this will be helpful to you. And that seeing how funny we can look on the courts will both amuse and outrage you, either of which ought to send you flying back to your instructor.

For all of you—the defective, the remedial and the mediocre, playing on grass, clay and cement courts throughout the country—I'd like to leave you with two gifts. One a secret and the other a warm thought. The secret (given to me by Fred Stolle who teamed with Ken Rosewall to be one of the most respected doubles around) is how to win a Pro Celebrity Match.

"Mr. Cosby." he said, "the best way to play a pro match is for you to stand over there by the net, keep yourself in ready position and never swing at anything unless it's going to hit you. In other words, keep out of your partner's way."

The warm thought, the one I like to mull over every now and then is, however high the cost of rackets, tennis shorts, shirts, sweaters, shoes, socks, lessons, camps, balls, sweat bands or club fees—remember there is one item that will always cost the same: the jockstrap.

ABOUT THE AUTHOR: Bill Cosby was born in Philadelphia in 1937 to William and Anna Cosby. He attended Wister Elementary School along with his brothers Bob and Russell, and his pals, Fat Albert, Old Weird Harold and a host of others made famous in his comedy routines. Sports and comedy have dominated Cosby's life ever since the days he played ball in the downtown projects of Philadelphia. His entrance to Temple University was made possible by an athletic scholarship. And it was at Temple, where he supported himself by tending bar, that he began to polish his talent as a comedian. His first stage appearance was at a club called The Underground. From there he has gone on to Emmy awards and Grammys. He has appeared in night clubs from Las Vegas to Greenwich, Reno to Lake Tahoe. Cosby is a Ph.D. candidate in education at Amherst, and is as active in educational programs as he is in Celebrity Tennis.